ABC

of flowers

To Ellie, James, Jack and Holly

My dear great-grandchildren

With all my love

from Grandee

2011

To my wonderful family, who all love flowers

MEMOIRS

Published by Memoirs Books

Memoirs Books

25 Market Place, Cirencester, Gloucestershire, GL7 2NX

www.memoirsbooks.co.uk

info@memoirsbooks.co.uk

Edited by Chris Newton
Book jacket design and layout Ray Lipscombe

ISBN
978-1-908223-12-8

Printed in England

Anemone

"Anemone" we say with care
A letter's here that should be there!
"Anemone" – yes, that's much better
You have to practise every letter!

Bluebell

Pretty bluebell, tall and slim
Blue carpet in the green woods dim
In Maytime woods she's strong and tall
But in a vase her petals fall.

Cowslip

Yellow cowslip blooms with grace
In many a springtime country place
Her name's the strangest I recall
She doesn't look like a cow at all.

Daisy

Pretty daisy shakes her head

She doesn't want to go to bed

In the morning when she wakes

To show her face an hour she takes.

Elderflower

Elderflower brightens hedges

Berries black along the edges

Wine she makes for Christmas cheer

Will keep until another year.

Forget-me-not

A pretty flower, small and blue

In springtime and in summer too

In flowerbeds and rockeries

You'll blossom where and when you please.

Gladioli

Gladioli, tall and strong
In pretty colours stands along
The pathway leading to the gate
Handsome, noble, tall and straight.

Hyacinth

Hyacinth with smell so sweet
Good to smell, though not to eat
Arranged along the window sill
To cheer us up when we are ill.

Iris

Her blue or yellow flowerheads

Tower above the flower beds

We place them at the back to show

That they will grow and grow and grow.

SUMMER   WINTER

Jasmine

Jasmine's spiky yellow flowers

Shine through winter's darkest hours

Brightening up the bleakest day

Till once again spring's on the way.

Kingcups

The kingcup shines in country ponds

In early spring we see her fronds

So bright they shine in colours bold

They're sometimes called marsh marigold.

Lupin

Lupins tall and stately stand
Along the wall they look so grand
When pretty butterflies alight
The lupin's such a pretty sight.

Marigold

Marigolds, their heads a-cluster

Remind us of a yellow duster

Bright and fluffy, but do not pick me

My smell will make you feel quite sickly!

Nasturtium

Nasturtiums make a pretty bower
Hung from a basket in a shower
Give them string to coil upon
They'll climb and climb towards the sun.

Orange blossom

Orange blossom's on the scene

In every young bride's wedding dream

Somewhere she's sure to wear a spray

To crown her very special day.

Pansy

Pansies, sweet with upturned faces

Thrive in oh so many places

Purple, yellow, orange too

They make the garden bright for you.

Queen of the May

May blossom used to make a crown

A maypole too, to dance around

Pretty girls to choose as Queen

The best Mayday we've ever seen

Rose

The scent of roses fills the air
Making perfume fine and rare
In a jar place each dropped petal
Cover with water, let them settle
Leave to stand for weeks to come
Around your jar the bees will hum.

Sunflower

The sunflower tall is hard to miss

It reaches high the sun to kiss

To screen a shed, a wall or fence

Such pretty cover, with no expense!

Tulip

Tulips make a splendid show

Standing nobly in a row

They do not like to grow inside

But give them a sheltered spot to hide

And they will thrive and bloom for sure

This year, next year, maybe more.

Umbrellas

The bindweed is its usual name
But here's a happy childhood game
Pick one, hold it like a brolly
It makes your walks to school so jolly!

Violet

Violets are such plucky flowers
They're first in spring to brave the showers
They grow just inches off the ground
They hide so well they're rarely found.

Wallflower

Wallflower sweet on old stone wall

How can you grow there at all?

Blooming orange, yellow, gold

Your roots must find it hard to hold.

X marks the spot

You've found a little packet
Of seeds you had forgot
Could they be lupins, lavender
Lobelia, or what?
Plant them in the garden
Mark where your seedbed lies
Then wait to see what they might be
Your summertime surprise.

Yellow daffodils

Yellow daffs in bloom a-plenty

In springtime woods which were so empty

Wintertime has been so drear

But now at last the spring is here

The woodlands fill with golden light

A scene of daffodil delight.

Zeal

The zeal with which we care for flowers

Working hard outside for hours;

The patience when we dig and hoe

The aches we suffer, head to toe;

The love we show for growing things

Are worth far more than diamond rings.

www.ingramcontent.com/pod-product-compliance
Lightning Source LLC
Chambersburg PA
CBHW042118040426

42449CB00002B/84